176 Nevers to Remember

By:
Kirksey Todd

The Sacred Name Edition with bonus Commentary

By:
Kirksey & Lolita Todd

**All Praises to YeHoWaH
The Most High!**

**The Elohim of Our Fathers
Abraham, Isaac, And Jacob!**

176 Nevers to Remember
The Sacred Name Edition with Bonus Commentary
All Rights Reserved
Copyright © 2016 by Kirksey & Lolita Todd

All rights reserved. No part of this publication may be reproduced, stored in a retrieval system, or transmitted in any form or by any means without prior permission of the publisher, except for brief reviews in magazines, or as quotations in another work when full attribution is given.

All Scripture references and quotations are taken from the King James Version (KJV) of the Bible.

PRINTED IN THE UNITED STATES OF AMERICA

ISBN: 978-0-9834191-1-2

Library of Congress Catalog Control Number: 2016958071

Published By
Divine Global Connections, LLC.
1.470-514-5076

176 Nevers to Remember
The Sacred Name Edition with Bonus Commentary
All Rights Reserved
Copyright © 2016 by Kirksey & Lolita Todd

First Edition
176 Nevers to Remember
Copyright ©2013
Kirksey Todd
Published By
Divine Global Connections, LLC.
www.divineglobalpublishing.com

Dedications

This work is dedicated to **YeHoWaH** our Elohim, the God of our fathers Abraham, Isaac, and Jacob. And to our five beautiful children;
Christopher, Kristen, Elisha, Elijah, Jordan and our beautiful grandson Adrian Isaiah Scott.

We love you all deeply.

Kirksey Todd aka **Yah-El Ben Yehudah**
&
Lolita A. Todd aka **Sarah ShemaYah Bat Yehudah**

Special Note:

As a Torah-observant Israelite, I believe that **YeHoWaH** is God and beside Him, there is no other. Because of this, it is my desire to present this Sacred Name Edition and the wisdom I have gleaned from the Torah, the standard for which I and my household live by.

Yah-El Ben Yehudah

Table of Contents

Forward
Lolita A. Todd

Introduction
Kirksey Todd

I. 110 Nevers to Remember – Page 2

II. 40 Nevers Men Must Remember Regarding Relationships – Page 32

III. 21 Nevers Women Must Remember Regarding Relationships – Page 43

IV. 5 Nevers Children Must Remember – Page 49

Forward

In 2013 the first edition of this amazing book was released. It was a first for both Yah-EL and I, his first published work as an Author and my first release as an Editor and Publisher. We were so excited, thankful and grateful to **YeHoWaH** for allowing both of us to experience having our shared dream come to pass. Well, the same holds true for this newly revised release of **176 Nevers to Remember: *The Sacred Name Edition*.** We are humbled by the opportunity to write and publish a work that celebrates and honors the name of the God of our Fathers Abraham, Isaac, and Jacob; **YeHoWaH**.

This revised edition of **176 Nevers to Remember** not only includes the beautiful sacred name of **YeHoWaH** our God, but it also includes commentary written by both Yah-El and I. We spent hours collaborating and discussing how these 176 tidbits of wisdom could impact the lives of those that read them. In the end, our goal was to present a practical and applicable understanding that expounds on the meaning of each "Never" in the context of everyday relational situations that impacts the lives of men, women and even children.

Lastly, you don't have to be a bible scholar or deeply spiritual to enjoy the benefits of this book. Yah-El wrote these "Nevers" for all ages and for every level of learning with the goal of stimulating a hunger for more of the knowledge, wisdom, and understanding found in the source by which this book was written and that is the Torah; Our constitution and the standard by which we live.

May this book offer insight, direction and practical understanding for your everyday living and remember it's for the entire family.

Shalom, Love and Blessings,
Lolita Todd aka Sarah ShemaYah Bat Yehudah
Publisher, Editor & Author
Divine Global Connections, LLC.

Introduction

Some of you may be asking, why a sacred name edition and what name are you referring to in the first place? I am referring the name of the Creator of the heavens and the earth; I am referring to the God of our forefathers Abraham, Isaac, and Jacob.

The Name of the Creator has been recorded almost 7,000 times in the Hebrew Scriptures alone. Now, I do not mean to offend anyone, but I must inform you that His name is not Jesus or Allah. Many people believe that Jesus is God in the flesh or the second person of the godhead in human form. There are many things wrong with this concept. First, God is not a man, most importantly, God cannot die. Lastly, Jesus himself never said he was God, his words, and actions such as praying contradict that thought. As for the word Allah, in the Arabic version of the Hebrew scriptures, the word Allah means "The Power or The God" So Allah is used to refer to the God of the Israelites.

At the burning bush, our Creator made Himself known by His name to our teacher Moses (Moshe). Moshe asked The Creator for His name to present to the people and this is what He said:

And God said unto Moses, I AM THAT I AM: and he said, Thus shalt thou say unto the children of Israel, I AM hath sent me unto you. And God said moreover unto Moses, Thus shalt thou say unto the

children of Israel, The LORD God of your fathers, the God of Abraham, the God of Isaac, and the God of Jacob, hath sent me unto you: this is my name for ever, and this is my memorial unto all generations. Exodus 3:14,15 KJV

Below are a few additional verses that you should read. Also, you should make a note to remember, whenever you see LORD or GOD in all capitals it is referring to the four-letter name of The Creator **Y-H-W-H**. By adding vowels, this enables us to pronounce His name which is, **YeHoWaH**. Please also note there are other variations of the sacred name used throughout the world.

   Exodus 9:16   Psalms 91:14,15   Psalms 95:1
   Proverbs 18:10   Isaiah 45:20-25   Isaiah 52:6

Shalom, Love & Blessings
Kirksey Todd aka **Yah-El Ben Yehudah**

Part I

110 **Nevers** to Remember

1. **N**ever forget that YeHoWaH has already made known our identity within the pages of the Torah.

   ➤   Knowledge of self is only possible by searching the Torah that teaches us about ourselves and our requirements to **YeHoWaH**.

2. **N**ever allow yourself to be put back to sleep by that which YeHoWaH has graciously awakened you from.

   ➤   When **YeHoWaH** has worked a work in your life and has liberated you from your past bondages. Do not allow yourself to fall again into the exact same trappings.

3. **N**ever speak of embracing a new year with the arms of the previous ones.

   ➤   When moving forward in life never allow yourself to think with last year's mindset. The failed plans of last year should never see the light of your new beginning.

4. **N**ever believe a famine can stop YeHoWaH from blessings you.

➢ **YeHoWaH is bigger than any setback that you may be experiencing at this moment. So, always remember the blessings of YeHoWaH comes with YeHoWaH.**

5. **Never see yourself as not being who you are because others will not recognize you as such.**

➢ Be true to who you are based on what **YeHoWaH** has revealed to you about you. Your true self is not based on the opinions of mere man.

6. **Never allow yourself, to be beaten in the game of life by your own hand.**

➢ One of the greatest setbacks in life is when we destroy our own destiny by not loving ourselves enough.

7. **Never miss a day at trying to be the best before the face of YeHoWaH our Elohim.**

➢ When we arise in the morning we should always strive to be the best that we can be, since He blessed us with another day. So, let's use our time wisely that we have upon the earth.

8. **Never allow life to abort the Torah that is written within your heart.**

➢ As humans, we go through all types of issues that can take our breath away, but we cannot allow those moments to steal the Torah from us as well.

9. **Never allow anything in life to hinder you from sharing the gifts that are within you.**

➢ Sometimes people get hurt so bad that they withdraw themselves from society, causing the community to miss out on the blessings within them.

10. **Never permit the death of other people's dreams to allow yours to die as well.**

➢ You may believe that others are more deserving than you are, and if they couldn't make their dreams come true, then perhaps yours will not either. But, you are not them, you are you. Their failures shouldn't become yours.

11. **Never reach out to help, when you know you won't stretch out to reach!**

➢ Do not play with people's emotions when they are in need. If you are not sincere about helping them, do not offer it.

12. **Never network with someone who doesn't know how to work their nets!**

➢ In both business and personal relationships, always surround yourself with like-minded people that are willing to put in the work, so that both will grow and be successful.

13. Never offer anything to YeHoWaH that you no longer desire to keep yourself.

➢ What we offer as a sacrifice to **YeHoWaH** should be our best. Normally, we desire to keep our best because we see the benefits of having it. Nevertheless, our love for **YeHoWaH** should outweigh what we desire to keep.

14. Never forget to come back and give thanks to YeHoWaH for His goodness.

➢ Never get so caught up in the blessings of **YeHoWaH**, that you forget to praise Him for the kindness He has bestowed.

15. Never think your true worth is based on your credit score.

➢ A poor credit score should not cause us to fall into a state of depression. Our value is not based on a man-made scoring system. It's based on **YeHoWaH's** system, which is found in His Torah.

16. Never allow un-repented sin to sit too close.

➢ It is wisdom to approach **YeHoWaH** with a re-pented heart, instead of sin as your companion before His throne.

17. Never see Jesus as YeHoWaH or equal to Him!

➢ There are many people that see Jesus as **YeHoWaH** and this provokes Him to jealousy. Therefore, let us stop giving **YeHoWaH**'s glory to another and return to **YeHoWaH** and to Him alone.

18. Never say or even think YeHoWaH can't redeem his people when He has already declared He can!

➢ As our Redeemer, **YeHoWaH** has promised to redeem His people. Just because you have not yet seen the full deliverance of His people, does not mean He has forgotten or that He will not do it. It is recorded that He is your Redeemer; you must believe that with all your heart even if you do not live to see it.

19. Never go forward when YeHoWaH is standing still!

➤ In life, sometimes we must slow down or come to a complete stop. We should never put ourselves into a situation that **YeHoWaH** is not a part of. Always have the approval of **YeHoWaH** before moving forward.

20. **N**ever **confuse backing up with giving up!**

➤ It is wisdom to sometimes step back to reexamine the instructions given by **YeHoWaH** just to make sure we are still on course.

21. **N**ever **react to a delay as a denial by YeHoWaH!**

➤ Remember our father Abraham and the promise that **YeHoWaH** gave him concerning having a child with Sarah. We must learn to endure and wait on **YeHoWaH**.

22. **N**ever **think you can go before YeHoWaH and exalt another name before His face!**

➤ If you were asked to stand before royalty, would you address him using someone else's name? Not at all, especially since he has a name of his own. Our King of kings, **YeHoWaH** doesn't require the name of Jesus or any other name to be used as a password to come into His presence, to seek His face or to ask for His help.

23. Never stand before YeHoWaH without bowing first!

➢ Sometimes we as a people can become too familiar with **YeHoWaH**. In fact, it's foolish to think we no longer must honor our King because of the length of our journey. Our longevity does not entitle us to become common with the Holy One of Israel.

24. Never present a gift that YeHoWaH will not accept!

➢ **YeHoWaH** has made it clear, what is good and acceptable to give to Him. We cannot give to **YeHoWaH** what is not approved by **YeHoWaH**.

25. Never think you can honor YeHoWaH by dishonoring His Torah!

➢ Many people talk about how much they love and honor **YeHoWaH**, but as soon as we speak of keeping His Commandments, they come up with reasons why they do not have too. **YeHoWaH** said to keep them, so it is wisdom to follow **YeHoWaH** and not man.

26. Never forget that YeHoWaH honors obedience over belief!

➢   **YeHoWaH** is more concerned with our obedience toward Him, than our belief in Him. Belief is a system governed by men, obedience is a requirement governed by **YeHoWaH**.

27. Never sow seeds in a field that produces only dead things.

➢   If you know something is no good, why would you waste your time with it? An investor would not invest money into a company going out of business because there is no hope for an ongoing return.

28. Never grant access to your heart to one known for breaking them!

➢   If someone is no good for you, why go through the process of having a relationship with them? Instead, save yourself the unnecessary heartache and pain.

29. Never say "I will" when your heart is full of "I will not"!

➢   It is easy to simply say what you mean and mean what you say. Stop pretending to be someone that you're not.

30. **Never consult with the mirror of man to see how you look to YeHoWaH!**

➢ People can tell you how you look to them, but not how you look to **YeHoWaH**, because **YeHoWaH** looks upon the heart.

31. **Never see yourself in a place of famine but in the storehouse of YeHoWaH!**

➢ You may lack financial success in the natural, but are rich spiritually. Instead, see yourself rich in **YeHoWaH**, and watch your natural state reflect it in time.

32. **Never wish to do over that which cannot be undone, just do not do over that which was!**

➢ Learn from your mistakes and strive to never do them again. Do not waste your time by wishing for a do-over.

33. **Never tell someone you will help them when you know you will not!**

➢ Be true to yourself. If it's not in your heart to help, do not say that you will.

34. Never climb a flight of stairs looking backward!

➢ When you make the decision to move forward, do it and don't look back. Looking back may cost you your future. Remember Lot's wife.

35. Never confuse patiently waiting with doing nothing!

➢ When **YeHoWaH** tells us to wait on Him, He is not telling us to sit on our butts and do nothing. Instead, keep his commandments, precepts, statutes and instructions as we wait on Him.

36. Never speak about what you do not have, but speak on that which YeHoWaH has said, "Can be!"

➢ Father Abraham was a perfect example for us concerning this. He gained strength standing on the promises that **YeHoWaH** gave him.

37. Never worry about your cares, just pray to YeHoWaH concerning them!

➢ Events in life can sometimes produce stress, worry and even lead to sickness. Pray to **YeHoWaH** and continue to live life the best that you can.

38. **N**ever think of YeHoWaH as "He was, for He is!

➢ Some people believe that **YeHoWaH** has changed, for example, they think He no longer does miracles for his people, but **YeHoWaH** is still the same yesterday, today and forevermore.

39. **N**ever allow an event, a moment, a mistake, or a sin to define who you really are!

➢ Do not allow the past to haunt you and keep you from being who you are in **YeHoWaH**.

40. **N**ever reveal a secret to one who doesn't love you.

➢ Not everyone is trustworthy to bear a secret that you hold dear. Wisdom teaches that we should know those we share our secrets with and we must be sure they have our best interest at heart.

41. **N**ever feel you cannot give, because you do not have money; for money is the lowest of things to give!

➢ The lack of money does not hinder one from being a giver because the greatest of things to give is one's self.

42. Never discard the gift because you dislike the container.

➢   **YeHoWaH** has always placed great treasure in the vessels that He has chosen to be a part of redemption, so overlook what you see with your eyes to see without them.

43. Never be too quick to say what is or isn't YeHoWaH!

➢   One that lacks knowledge has no right to judge righteously. One that lacks understanding cannot explain, and one that forsakes Torah has no true wisdom at all.

44. Never proclaim to speak for YeHoWaH, when you can't hear his voice.

➢   A true student that desires to teach, must be able to always hear the voice of his Teacher, who is **YeHoWaH**. If you can't hear the voice of the Teacher, don't be fooled, having the Teacher's manual will not help.

45. Never confess to loving YeHoWaH when you choose to be disobedient to Him at the same time!

➢ Lips of praise alone will not get you to the next level, you must have willing obedience as well.

46. **Never expect much from a cracked glass!**

➢ Many times, damaged people will damage others, so **YeHoWaH** must repair the glass first so we can enjoy that which He has poured into it.

47. **Never be angry about not reaching your goals, be angry about having no goals to reach!**

➢ The deadline was missed, the completion date may have been pushed back, but production has not been halted, so hope remains.

48. **Never be upset about not having a big house, if the home you have is big in love!**

➢ A family unit that loves one another is as a family that owns a mansion. The size of the house does not make it a home, the love between the family does.

49. **Never just plan to sleep, but also plan to dream dreams!**

➢ Dreams are important because they help forge the path to destiny. **YeHoWaH** will sometimes use our dreams to lead and guide us along the way, so keep dreaming.

50. Never ever forget that YeHoWaH, the Lord of heaven and earth made you for His purpose!

➢ Most people do not have hope because they feel they have no purpose in life. Therefore, they go through life aimlessly. When we connect with **YeHoWaH** our true purpose is made known.

51. Never select a place of worship because the members appear to be nice, the music is good and the building is beautiful.

➢ The above alone cannot be the sole reason for gathering together. Our selection should be for learning to do, studying to teach, and for building a nation.

52. Never select a mentor who isn't sitting where you desire to sit.

➢ Surrounding ourselves with people that we can look up to and learn from is very important.
Remember, the mentor that you choose should challenge you to dig for the wealth hidden inside of them.

53. Never choose a mate based on the gifts they give.

➢ When we choose to be with a person it should not be based on their income or upon the many things that they can do for us financially. It should solely be based on their character.

54. Never sow seed where the harvest cannot be accounted for.

➢ Don't pour your gifts, talents, and money into anything that cannot be justified or explained. If you can't explain the reason for your investment. Someone may not be able to explain the reason for a lack of return.

55. Never allow a misunderstanding to dissolve a successful partnership.

➢ In every relationship, there will be moments of disagreement, but that's no reason to dissolve a successful merger that produces a continual profit.

56. Never stand someone up who is willing to pick you up.

➢ When we encounter someone or a group that is willing to help us reach our goals in life, we should never take them for granted or overlook their wisdom.

57. Never engage in a battle that YeHoWaH has not ordained.

➢ **YeHoWaH** can be with you or against you, so it is very important to know where the Creator stands on certain issues pertaining to you.

58. Never allow the loss of an old love to hinder the arrival of the new.

➢ Breakups are very painful, but never think it is the end of the world. When we lose someone, it may be the beginning of something new.

59. Never permit a hot spot to cool you off, just keep moving forward with YeHoWaH.

➢ There will be good and bad days in life, but we should never lose heart or give up on what we can be or what we can obtain.

60. Never allow your home to be known for folly, but allow it to be known for being a house of prayer and study.

➢ Your home is an extension of yourself. If you open your doors to all kinds of folly, then it's likely you'll open yourself to just about anything. **YeHoWaH** calls His house, a house of prayer for all nations. What is your home known for?

61. Never complain to YeHoWaH about the mate you have chosen, simply pray to YeHoWaH concerning them.

➢ It is important to keep your mate lifted in prayer before the face of **YeHoWaH**. When we complain about our mate, it's like committing them to their grave before their time.

62. Never build a great house on a foundation that cannot support it.

➢ The standard that you desire to teach should never be based solely on your feelings or on words taken out of context.

63. Never be sad with the departure of one that betrays you.

➢ Don't cry over the loss of one that betrays you. If **YeHoWaH** has moved that person out of your life, just know their replacement has probably been praying for a friend just like you.

64. Never be afraid to correct a wrong you have done.

➢ Always seize the opportunity to repair that which has been damaged by your words or actions.

65. Never give in to a bad situation that YeHoWaH can get you out of.

➢ Just ask the three Hebrew boys.

66. Never expose the secrets of a friend to gain another.

➢ It is not wisdom to betray a dear friend to try to get close to another one. Secrets are called secrets for a reason.

67. Never lose hope on issues that YeHoWaH never declared, will not be.

➢ The dreams that you have are still doable, especially if **YeHoWaH** is leading you toward the dream. However, the path that He may have chosen for you to obtain your dream, may be different from the one that you have chosen for yourself.

68. Never lose hope in YeHoWaH, when you are still among the living.

➢ We cannot become delusional when bad things happen in our lives. Nor, can we see setbacks as a form of death. While you yet still have breath hope remains.

69. Never lose sleep because of the loudness of the storm, remember it's just life's issues and it will pass.

➢ Life is just what it is, so do not lose heart. The sun will shine one day and a storm will come on another day. But, regardless of it all; **YeHoWaH** remains the same.

70. Never let the rules of baseball determine your walk before YeHoWaH.

➢ Like baseball, our justice system may say three strikes and you're out, but **YeHoWaH** will give us chance after chance to hit it out the park.

71. Never be eternally upset because you have fallen, just be thankful that you can get back up again.

➢ Spending time focused on the fall, the failure, the mistake or sin is a waste of time. It can rob you of your joy. Instead, focus on having a change of mind and getting back up.

72. **N**ever let a "no" stop you from moving toward your "yes."

➢ See #68.

73. **N**ever stop dreaming just because you had a nightmare.

➢ Some people have stopped dreaming because of a bad experience that was like a nightmare. You may be in a pit or jail one moment, and sitting in the seat of royalty the next. Don't give up on your dreams.

74. **N**ever disown the vows you made before YeHoWaH.

➢ Broken promises are only broken if you choose not to keep them. Time may have come and gone, but don't let time keep you from fulfilling your commitment. It's not too late.

75. **N**ever give up YeHoWaH's lifetime blessing for a moment of carnal bliss.

➢ Do not let the mindset of Esau cause you to lose your birthright.

76. **Never pass up the opportunity to get YeHoWaH's attention.**

➢ **YeHoWaH** is always watching and listening. So, remember to pray, worship, and praise Him in all things.

77. **Never permit what you have heard from others to rob you of what YeHoWaH has shown you.**

➢ **YeHoWaH** is only testing you, so do not lose hope of that which you can't see naturally, but can see spiritually.

78. **Never permit what you have seen to silence what YeHoWaH has spoken.**

➢ Seeing things that are contrary to what **YeHoWaH** has promised; is only a test given by **YeHoWaH**, so you can see what you are made of.

79. **Never dive head first into a pool to check the temperature, when you can simply use your feet.**

➢ In the game of life, it is easy to want to make a big splash and get everyone's attention. Sometimes it is better to take baby steps and feel your way around.

80. Never be a non-swimmer and jump into the deep end of the pool without a lifeguard on duty.

➢ Don't jump into big plans without the assistance and counsel of someone that has been there and done it long before you.

81. Never run with a pack that is running the wrong way.

➢ When you already know the right way to go, don't be influenced by the multitude of people running in the opposite direction.

82. Never give support to a foundation that does not give support.

➢ Many foundations claim to reach the four corners of the earth with aid and relief. They collect millions of dollars in donations promising to meet the needs of others. Before you support their endeavors, make sure they are accountable and their support is genuine.

83. Never quit on your goals because your team did, just get a new team.

➢ People that cannot see your vision or have your passion for life should not be allowed to feast on your drive for success.

84. Never stop running the race because another has broken the tape first.

➢ If you're in the race and others cross the finish line first. Don't let that stop you from crossing the finish line too. There may be a prize waiting on the other side that you cannot see.

85. Never extend a helping hand to one who you do not want to help.

➢ Don't offer to help, when you have no intentions to see it through. It is heartbreaking to have someone offer their assistance and not do it.

86. Never declare to one the way to go when you yourself have not gone all the way.

➢ It is impossible to mentor someone to a place that you have never been. First set and accomplish your goals. Only then can you help them to obtain theirs.

87. Never speak on the behalf of someone you do not know.

➢ You have worked with this person for a few months, been a neighbor to this other individual for a year and have met this other person in a social setting on various occasions. None of these qualifies as knowing them.

88. Never give instructions you will not follow yourself.

➢ A righteous teacher will do the righteousness that they teach their students.

89. Never give up on a race you can win, because your running mates have.

➢ In track and field, team events only require for one member to break the tape first. So, do not slow down because the rest of the team has.

90. Never think that the power is our prayers, remember our prayers are only connectors.

➢ Many people say that there is power in prayer, but prayer in and of itself is not the power; **YeHoWaH** is, and only true prayer will connect us to Him.

91. Never try to gain access into YeHoWaH's kingdom on someone else's passport.

➢ **YeHoWaH** will judge us based on our own merits, not on the righteousness of one individual.

92. Never allow a negative experience to keep you from experiencing YeHoWaH's goodness.

➢ You prayed and things didn't go as you hoped. Don't lose heart and refuse to keep coming to **YeHoWaH** because you didn't get your way. **YeHoWaH** is good and He has a plan.

93. Never allow incomplete work to make you quit working for YeHoWaH.

➢ Just because others have failed to complete their assignments, shouldn't cause us to not do our part for **YeHoWaH**.

94. Never make yourself out to be a trail-blazer and leave no trail to follow.

➢ A true teacher is only a good student that paid attention in class and have applied the lessons learned and can now show others the way to follow.

95. Never feel you cannot win because someone in a situation like yours didn't.

➤ Do not measure yourself against the failures of others, that is their story and not yours.

96. Never allow your shortcomings to cause you to miss your appointment with YeHoWaH.

➤ Learn to forgive yourself so that when **YeHoWaH** calls upon you to serve you will be ready.

97. Never spend time or money on that which will not better you.

➤ An investor is always looking for either a short or long-term return on their investment. The goal is to achieve a profit. The same applies to you. Invest wisely in yourself.

98. Never tell YeHoWaH to summon another when He has called you.

➤ **YeHoWaH** is the architect of all things. If He called you to do the job, then He knows you have what it takes to carry it out. So, trust Him above your own thoughts, feelings, and talent.

99. Never allow pride to keep you from admitting you do not know everything.

➢ Being a teacher does not mean that you know everything. This rule will open the door to knowing more.

100. Never say your relationship is solid when you and your spouse do not relate.

➢ Relating to each other means; staying true to one another, instead of creating false imagines of what your relationship is not.

101. Never give up because of a down season.

➢ In any kind of relationship, there will be ups and downs; Neither should stop us from moving forward.

102. Never speak a blessing or curse over someone or something that YeHoWaH has spoken contrary of.

➢ Remember the story of Balaam.

103. Never underestimate the power of YeHoWaH.

➢ Duh!

104. Never close off your mind to the creative thoughts of YeHoWaH concerning you.

➢ Meditating on the thoughts of **YeHoWaH** can change how you see yourself and save your life.

105. Never allow a lie concerning YeHoWaH to become your truth!

➢ We have many people that have come to believe so many falsehoods concerning **YeHoWaH**, these untruths will not help us in our redemption.

106. Never think the only way to YeHoWaH is through the man called Jesus!

➢ The ancient ways and requirements of our fathers did not include Jesus. Abraham our Father and Moses our Teacher never knew him or even called on his name for anything.

107. Never assume that your path to YeHoWaH is the only one!

➢ We must remember the only way to **YeHoWaH** is the way of Torah.

108. Never assume you cannot because others could not.

➢ Do not measure yourself against other people, be your own person.

109. Never let leadership lead you down the wrong path.

➢ We must be willing to fact check that which we are taught. Taking what is being taught without question or study because it came from a leader only proves you are just a follower.

110. Never allow leadership to become YeHoWaH in your life!

➢ When we make a man equal to **YeHoWaH**, we cross the line into idolatry.

Part II

40 **<u>Nevers</u> <u>Men</u>** Must Remember Regarding Relationships

111. **Never pursue a woman that belongs to another.**

➢ Simple wisdom!

112. **Never pursue a woman that doesn't want to be caught by you.**

➢ Respect the wishes of the lady that you desire because in the future it's your character she will remember.

113. **Never give up the pursuit just because you already have her.**

➢ What it took to get her, it will take that and more to keep her.

114. **Never allow life to ruin the life you and your spouse have started together.**

➢ In relationships, there are moments where things may not go right, but always remember the covenant that you have entered into before **YeHoWaH**.

115. **Never look at the woman you have and see the one that you had.**

➢ Duh!

116. N ever look at the woman you have and see the one you want.

➢ See #5.

117. N ever nourish a flower that refuses to bloom.

➢ Many men try to buy a woman's love because she will not give it freely. If you bankrupt yourself to gain her love. Then her love will always be in question.

118. N ever sow seeds of love on a field that only produces thorns.

➢ She has already shown she is not interested. She is cold and **YeHoWaH** has not given his stamp of approval. Why continue, you are only asking to be pricked.

119. N ever reveal the secrets of your spouse to a friend.

➢ That which is between you and your wife stays between you and your wife. Don't disclose what she has not authorized.

120. Never kiss the lips of one dipped in poison.

➤ Her lips are filled with kind words, her appearance is breathtaking, but with a listening ear and eyes that look beyond the obvious, you can see the dangerous woman that she really is.

121. Never stop trying to win her heart even though you already won it.

➤ If you have wined and dined her in the past, don't stop. Otherwise, she may seek attention elsewhere.

122. Never hold the hand of one who will not hold yours back.

➤ It is not wise to pursue an unaffectionate woman if you require a certain degree of intimacy. Initially, the pursuit may be fun, but in the long run what you catch will not be what you want.

123. Never pledge your undying love to someone who will try to kill it.

➤ Choose wisely those you make a pledge and a vow with, because a commitment made to the wrong person may cost you more than money.

124. Never expose the ring before the hand is ready to wear it.

➤ You may be ready for marriage, but before presenting the ring, make sure she can fit it.

125. Never hold a grudge against the one you love.

➤ Holding a grudge is like holding the bottom of a hot pan that contains a fine meal. Instead of letting go, your burning yourself and missing out on what is on the inside.

126. Never order a bed made for two if you have not become one first.

➤ Get married.

127. Never waste time in the pursuit of another man's woman even if she isn't faithful.

➤ It is not wise to go after a woman who is with someone else. Nor is it wise to think she'll be faithful to you when she couldn't with him.

128. Never think the purchase of a house will make it a happy home.

➢ Buying nice things doesn't guarantee a loving relationship.

129. Never be fooled to think because you like the same things that you would like each other.

➢ Having the same taste in music, clothes, and friends doesn't mean that you should get involved.

130. Never be fooled to think because you don't like the same things that you will not like each other.

➢ Remember, sometimes opposites do attract.

131. Never place the title of savior on your children regarding your relationship.

➢ Do not put that kind of pressure on your kids to save what is destined to fail.

132. Never think because you both love children that you should have some.

➢ A person that likes or even loves being around kids does not mean that they are qualified to be a parent.

133. Never propose to a woman until you know that she's indeed your wife.

➢ You should only go shopping for a ring because you know that she'll accept it.

134. Never perceive she is a good woman because she did a good thing.

➢ Good deeds have their place and even the worst of the worst can do something good. Generally, the motive behind the deed is what a wise person will examine. Look at the motive, not just the deed.

135. Never allow the glory of her appearance to blind you from seeing the true her.

➢ As a man, you cannot allow her physical beauty to be the deciding factor for pursuing her.

136. Never declare she is your helpmeet, yet won't help you to make ends meet.

➢ This is not based so much on just having a job, but a willingness to be a support in all things.

137. Never ask a woman to commit to your vision when YeHoWaH is not even in your sight.

➢ A man who longs for a wife should be a man that has **YeHoWaH** in his life.

138. **N**ever confuse having good times with having a good relationship.

➢ Two or three good days out of a week doesn't mean she is a sure thing or very promising.

139. **N**ever hug a choker.

➢ Any sign of abusive behavior is an indicator to grab your tzitzit (fringes) and RUN.

140. **N**ever think that relocating will help you in relating to your mate.

➢ Many people fool themselves into thinking that they can restore the fire in their relationship simply by moving somewhere else. If the problem is within you, then it will travel with you. First, be healed and then move on.

141. **N**ever confuse giving gifts to your spouse with offering yourself.

➢ Most women love receiving nice things, but a real woman wants to have the true gift, which is you.

142. Never be afraid to reveal your wounds to the woman you love.

➢ It is hard for men to come clean about their painful past, but if you have a good woman, allow her to help in the process of your healing.

143. Never believe there are secrets worth keeping from the one you love.

➢ There may be things from your past that are shameful, but it's a part of you. Therefore, be willing to share that part with her. A woman that loves you will continue to embrace you regardless of your history.

144. Never allow the smile of a beautiful stranger, cause you to lose focus.

➢ We should never be blinded by someone's beauty that we lose sight of issues that really matter and most importantly **YeHoWaH**.

145. Never think you're a weak man because you ran from a powerful woman.

➢ Running from a woman may be necessary; remember Joseph and follow his lead.

146. Never lower your observance of YeHoWaH's standards to have a beautiful woman.

➢ If you are a Ten Commandments type of guy, don't desire a woman so bad, that you're willing to become a follower of seven commandments to have her.

147. Never hold on too tight to one who wants to be free, you may push them away for good.

➢ Trust is a major pillar in every relationship. If you don't allow your mate personal space and freedoms that are within reason, you run the risk of losing them.

148. Never let the death of your relationship mean the death of all things.

➢ Some people cannot move on after a bad relationship or the loss of a loved one. You are not dead, now LIVE!

149. Never allow your acts of immaturity to stop you from becoming a man of YeHoWaH.

➢ Just because you have made some foolish decisions in your life, does not mean that you can't grow up to embrace the GOD consciousness of our fathers.

150. **N**ever **think just because you both believe in YeHoWaH that your relationship is destined to work.**

➢ Belief alone does not make a relationship work. you must work the works that will make a relationship successful.

Part III

21 <u>Nevers</u> <u>Women</u> Must Remember Regarding Relationships

151. Never pursue a man, instead allow him to pursue you.

➢ Being found by the right man is based on your virtue.

152. Never assume he is godly just because he believes in YeHoWaH.

➢ Saying the right thing does not mean that he lives the right way.

153. Never believe every door opener and every chair puller is a gentleman.

➢ A pretender can only pretend for so long and a man that wears a mask will eventually have to take it off. Therefore, watch and wait.

154. Never lay in bed with a man that is not your husband.

➢ When you're single, the bed is for sleeping, but when you're married the bed is a place of intimacy.

155. Never be led by a man that has no vision.

➢ Never settle for a man that does not have his sights on **YeHoWaH** and making you happy.

156. Never let his muscles decide your future.

➢ Big muscles do not mean that he has a big heart and that he has a plan in place to impact your life for the good.

157. Never let a handsome man blow your mind.

➢ The physical appearance of a man can turn heads, but never allow it to turn your heart from **YeHoWaH**.

158. Never allow a man's job to be your main reason for dating him.

➢ A lewd man can have a nice job, so don't be fooled by it. A nice job does not mean he is a nice man.

159. Never accept a date with a man that cannot set a date to meet your parents, children or your GOD.

➢ A real man is willing to sit down with those that are important to you and have helped to define who you are.

160. Never date a man that is not willing to include your children.

➢ A real man wants to spend time with your children even when you're not around.

161. Never allow that one mistake to become a life sentence.

➢ Sometimes we can be haunted by the ghost of a bad decision from the past, but never allow the dead body to dwell in your heart or in your home.

162. Never move in with a man until your last name matches his.

➢ Commentary not needed.

163. Never think he can change your life if he can't help change diapers.

➢ If he is willing to share his name, a bed and make some children. Then sharing the responsibilities of parenting is included.

164. Never say "I do" to a man that only says, "I can't."

➢ A great relationship is not based on someone always getting their way, it must consist of moments of compromise.

165. Never overlook a good man because he did a bad thing.

➢ He was labeled a criminal, a failure, a liar, and an all-around loser. Those were his ways many years ago, but he has since changed. Don't allow his past to keep you from embracing who he is now.

166. Never let a bad man into your home because he did a good thing.

➢ He helped you in your time of need, but he is known for his bad behavior. So, don't allow one act of kindness to persuade you to give him access to your home or to your heart.

167. Never think because you decided to keep the baby, that you must keep the father as well.

➢ Countless marriages have been founded solely on the birth of a child. These relationships are generally absent of true friendship and love and in the end, the child may suffer for it. You might not stay with the man, but do not deny the child the right to know their father in the process.

168. Never accept a proposal without a ring present.

➢ Any real man that is serious about you will have the ring on hand.

169. Never feel incomplete because you have no man in your life.

➢ A woman does not need a man to be complete. Remember **YeHoWaH** said, "It is not good for man to be alone", for he needs help to do what **YeHoWaH** called him to do.

170. Never allow a man to name you if you are not a part of him.

➢ Adam was qualified to name Eve because she was literally a part of him. Therefore, a woman walks beside the man, where the rib is and not behind him.

171. Never allow your desire for a mate to be equal with your desire for **YeHoWaH**.

➢ Anytime your longing for a man is equal or greater than your desire for **YeHoWaH** you now have a jealous GOD in your rearview mirror.

Part IV

5
<u>Nevers</u>
<u>Children</u>
Must Remember

172. **N**ever think that talking back to your parents proves you are grown, it only shows you are still a child.

➤ Commentary not needed.

173. **N**ever take the instructions of your father or mother lightly, for YeHoWaH doesn't.

➤ **YeHoWaH** is listening and watching you. He is measuring your level of obedience to Him by how you honor your parents.

174. **N**ever do what your friends are doing if it goes against the instructions of YeHoWaH and your parents.

➤ Peer pressure is a term that means being pressured or negatively influenced by those within your age group. Whenever someone influences you to do the opposite of what **YeHoWaH** or your parent's command, they are not your friend.

175. **N**ever bring shame to the name of YeHoWaH or break the heart of your parents.

➤ Any child that identifies themselves as a child of **YeHoWaH,** would not bring shame to His character. Nor trouble their parents by their actions

176. Never forget that the length of your days rides upon how you treat your parents.

➢ Respecting and honoring your parents is more than the words you say, it includes your actions when they're not around. Every time you walk honorably both in their presence and in their absence, it will add to your length of days.

NOTES

NOTES

NOTES

NOTES

NOTES

NOTES

176 Nevers to Remember

By:
Kirksey Todd

The Sacred Name Edition with bonus Commentary

By:
Kirksey & Lolita Todd

www.ingramcontent.com/pod-product-compliance
Lightning Source LLC
LaVergne TN
LVHW051512070426
835507LV00022B/3061